Contents

Making music together

There are many musical instruments in the world. Each instrument makes a different sound. We can make music together by playing these instruments in an **orchestra**. An orchestra is a large group of musicians.

Bands and orchestras are made up of different groups of instruments. One of these groups is called the string family. You can see many stringed instruments in this orchestra.

What are stringed instruments?

These are all stringed instruments. They have strings stretched over them. When the strings are played they **vibrate**. This makes a sound.

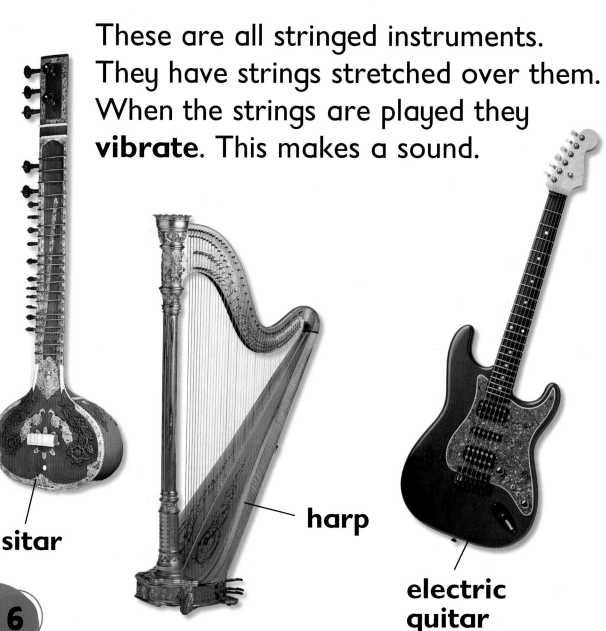

sitar

harp

electric guitar

bow

cello

You play some stringed instruments with a bow. A bow is a stick with strings stretched between the ends. The strings are made of horsehair or nylon.

You play others with a **plectrum** made of wood or plastic.

guitar

plectrums

The violin

The violin is a stringed instrument. Many children learn to play the violin when they are young. You may learn to play on a small violin first.

You can learn to play the violin in school. You can play the violin on your own. This is called playing **solo**.

Making a noise

The violin has four strings. It has a **curved** body. You play it with a bow. You move the bow across the strings to make a sound.

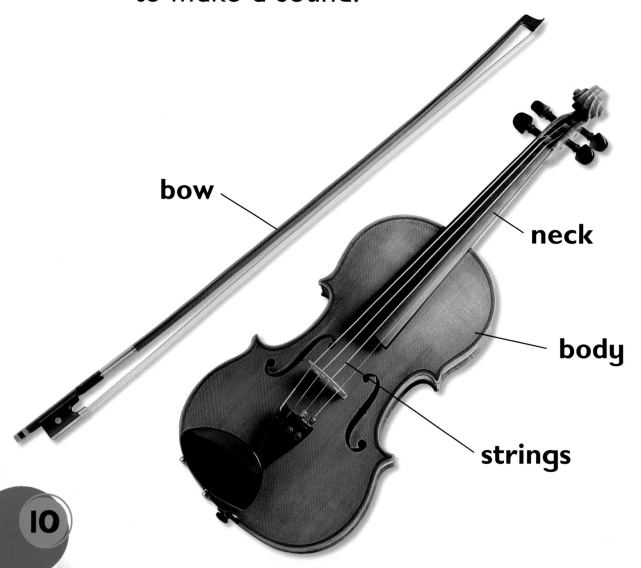

bow

neck

body

strings

You rub rosin into the part of the bow that touches the strings. Rosin is sticky stuff that comes from a tree. It helps the bow grip the string.

How the sound is made

The body of the violin is **hollow**. We call it a sound box. You move the bow across the strings to make a sound. This happens because the bow makes the strings **vibrate**. They move from side to side.

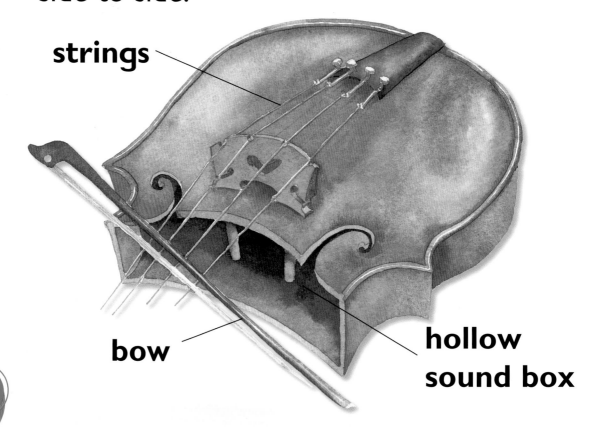

strings

bow

hollow sound box

This movement of the strings makes
the air in the sound box vibrate.
When air vibrates, it makes a sound.
You can press your fingers against the
strings to change the sound.

Types of strings

The viola looks like the violin but it is a bit bigger. It has a different **pitch** (sound). This is because the sound box is bigger than the one in the violin.

violin

viola

The cello is much larger than the violin. It sounds much lower. To play, you use a bow. You sit down and hold the cello between your knees.

Guitars

The guitar is a stringed instrument. You **strum** the guitar with your fingers. You can **pluck** it with a **plectrum**. To change the sound you press your fingers on the strings on the neck of the guitar.

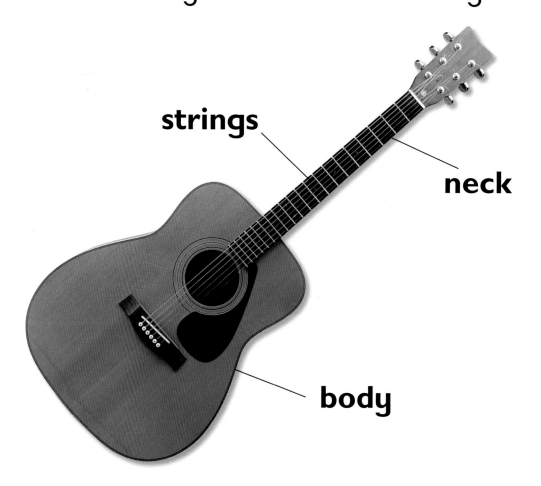

strings

neck

body

There are many different types of guitar. You can hear the steel guitar in **blues** and **folk music**. In **pop music**, you can hear the electric and bass guitar.

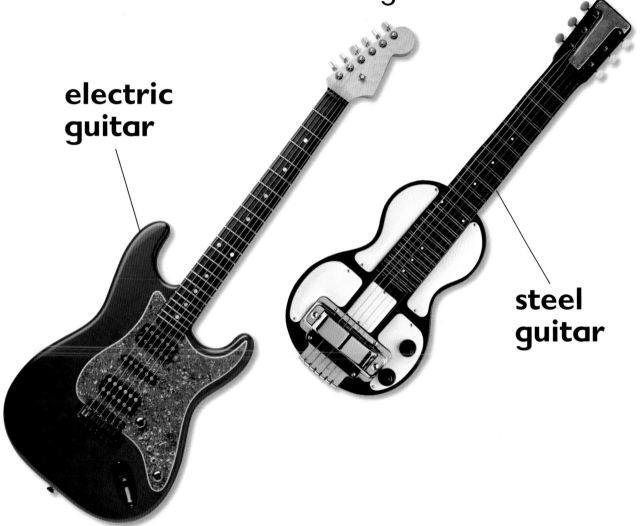

electric guitar

steel guitar

String concert

You may hear stringed instruments in a concert in school. In a string **quartet** (four musicians), you can hear the cello, two violins, and a viola.

Your teacher may play the guitar in school. These children are learning to sing a new song.

The wider family

The harp is a **curved** instrument with up to 48 strings. The harpist sits and **plucks** the strings. He plucks it from both sides of the harp.

You play the zither on a table.
You can also play it on your
lap.

Around the world

You can find stringed instruments all over the world. The sitar is from India. You **pluck** the strings with a wire **plectrum**.

The koto is an old instrument from Japan. Women often play the koto. They sit on the ground to play it. One end of the koto rests on their lap. The other end rests on the ground.

Famous musicians and composers

Nigel Kennedy is a famous musician. He is a violin player. He plays violin music written by famous **composers**.

Vivaldi is a famous composer. He composed (wrote) a lot of music for the violin. Kennedy plays Vivaldi's music.

Sarah Chang began to play the violin when she was four years old. When she was five, she played in her first **public** concert. She is a famous musician.

Music now

Today you can hear stringed instruments in **jazz**, **rock**, and Irish **folk music**. These people are playing Irish folk music.

You can hear people play electric guitars in rock and **pop music** today. You can also hear electric violins.

Sound activity

- You can make your own guitar.

- You will need an empty box. You will need four rubber bands and a pencil.

- Wide rubber bands make a low sound.

- Thin bands make a high sound.

- Stretch the four rubber bands over the box. Stretch them from end to end.

- This is the sound box.

- Place the pencil under the rubber bands next to the hole.

- **Pluck** your guitar!

Thinking about strings

You can find the answers to all of these questions in this book.

1. What is rosin? How do you use it?
2. What is a **plectrum**?
3. Which instruments play in a string **quartet**?
4. From which country is the sitar?

More books to read

Little Nippers: Making Music: Plucking, Angela Aylmore (Heinemann Library, 2005)

Musical Instruments of the World: Stringed Instruments, M. J. Knight (Franklin Watts Ltd, 2005)

Glossary

blues old style of slow, sad music from America

composed music that has been written

curved bent around

folk music old, traditional style of music from a place or country

hollow empty inside

jazz old style of music from the United States that is often made up as it is played

orchestra large group of musicians who play their musical instruments together
You say *ork-es-tra*

pitch the highness or lowness of a sound or musical note

plectrum small piece of wood or plastic used to pluck the strings of some stringed instruments

pluck pull

pop music music of the last 50 years. A lot of people like this music.

public open to all or lots of people

quartet group of four musicians or piece of music for four players
You say *kwoor-tet*

rock music kind of pop music with a strong beat

solo song or piece of music for one person

strum to pull fingers down over the strings of an instrument

vibrate move up and down or from side to side very quickly

Index